CIPRIAN NICOLAE

The 5 Steps Towards Fulfillment

Paintings by Delia Nicolae

Balboa Press books may be ordered through booksellers or by contacting:

Balboa Press
A Division of Hay House
1663 Liberty Drive
Bloomington, IN 47403
www.balboapress.com
844-682-1282

Interior Image Credit: Delia Nicolae

ISBN: 978-1-9822-6916-6 (sc)
978-1-9822-6915-9 (e)

Print information available on the last page.

Balboa Press rev. date: 05/19/2021

BALBOA.PRESS
A DIVISION OF HAY HOUSE

Table of Contents

"Whether you think you can, or you think you can't - you're right"

Henry Ford

FOREWORD

"The 5 steps towards Fulfillment" is a book written from a combination of personal experience, alongside lessons that I have learned from the experiences of those close to me, from the interviews and (auto) biographies of many famous people, and from the many personal development books I have been reading in the past 25 years.

The book represents the spiritualization of these experiences and lessons that I will be presenting in the following five chapters that correspond to the five steps that I believe we must climb in order to reach fulfillment.

The way I see things, fulfillment is much more important than success, whether it is a financial, professional, scientific, or notoriety success. A man can have success and yet not feeling fulfilled, and vice versa. A man can be unsuccessful by generally accepted standards and yet feeling fulfilled.

I tried to be direct and use plain speech more specific to oral expression than written as if we were having a discussion between friends.

"Opportunities don't happen; you create them."

Chris Grosser

WHAT IS SUCCESS?

For each and single one of us, success has a different meaning. In fact, success can have several different meanings, but one meaning, in particular, is what we consider essential, the one that, if we reach, we consider ourselves fulfilled.

Probably the most widespread meaning of success, the one many of us think about the most, and thus we say about someone that he/she is "a successful person," it has to do with financial success.

It is certainly an important criterion by which success can be defined, but is it the most

important?

It would be interesting to know how many of the people are perceived as being fulfilled because of their fortune truly feel fulfilled.

We know for sure that not all of them, because we hear about very rich people who openly confess that they feel unhappy, that their problems are a burden (and when we hear that, don't we think, "Why wouldn't I have his problems, alongside that kind of money"?), some even do suicide.

For others, success is defined by their career and by their professional achievements. Those achievements are often accompanied by financial success, but for some, this is not an (equally) important component. For those that consider their careers to be the most important aspect of success, to them, it matters what they do for a living, the fact that they have professional satisfaction, and the fact that they are appreciated for what they do in their profession.

Certainly, we all know or heard of people who stay up late at work, neglecting their families and never taking a break, because they have work to do and cannot detach themselves from their everyday work duties.

For others, success is all about notoriety. Sure, this comes hand in hand with the money, but for these people, what matters the most is to be recognized by others. I know people who get ecstatic like children if they are stopped on the street by fans for an autograph, for a selfie or if greeted on the street, people for whom these signs of celebrity and popularity are more important than anything else. I'm not saying that for them, it doesn't matter or they don't care about money, but they prefer notoriety first.

Finally, for others, success is personal - having a great family, friends to meet and go on vacation with, being able to come home worry-free or go out to a restaurant, to a movie, and to be relaxed. Sure, they want to have a certain financial level, but not necessarily above average. These people primarily prefer peace, relaxation and they are not willing to sacrifice themselves in exchange for a greater effort which would bring more money.

It's just like in the story when an American tourist stopped by on a Mexican seaside village.

One morning, he asks a Mexican to take him by boat when he goes fishing.

They go fishing, the Mexican catches some fish, and they return.

When they reached the shore, the American asked him:

"What are you going to do with these fish?"

"I am going take them home to my wife to cook them and eat them today," the Mexican replies.

"Why didn't you fish more, then?" asks the American.

"Because tomorrow I will go and fish more."

"You only fished for 2-3 hours; what do you do the rest of the time?"

"After I eat, I take a nap and sleep for 2-3 hours," answered the Mexican, *"and then, in the evening I will take my wife and go to the bar, where we will meet with our friends, we will drink something, we will eat something, we will talk, we will laugh, we will have a good time, then we will come back home and go to bed."*

"Look," says the American, *"I will teach you what to do: instead of just fishing 2 or 3 hours you stay at sea all day, you sell the fish that you don't need to the nearby stores and earn more money."*

"And what do I do with the money?" the Mexican asks.

"You save money and buy another boat, you hire someone, you fish more, and you earn even more money."

"And what do I do with that money?"

"You buy more boats; you hire more people, you buy some freezers, so you can sell to stores in the surrounding cities, and you will earn even more money."

"And what do I do with that money?"

"You expand internationally to the United States, and in 30 years, when the business will become big enough, you will list it on the stock exchange, you will sell it, and you will earn $ 100 million."

"And what do I do with that money?"

"With that money you retire and go to a village like this one, where you can buy a boat to go out with it on the sea for pleasure 2-3 hours a day, you fish enough to eat, then take a nap, and in the evening go to the bar, meet friends, eat something, drink something, talk and feel good."

After all, success should be a mix of all these factors, but it is up to each one of us to determine its proportions.

In any case, I believe that in order to be successful, five ingredients are needed. Possibly more, but I identified these five:

1. Vision

2. Determination

3. Perseverance

4. Balance

5. Gratitude

"If you can imagine it, you can achieve it."

William Arthur Ward

VISION

"Vision is a picture of the future that creates passion in people."

Bill Hybels

By vision, I mean the strategic goal, where we want to end up at when we reach an important milestone.

Vision is mandatory, from the very beginning, we must set a goal, an objective, a target that we want to follow; otherwise, no matter how hard we try, it would be in vain, and we end up wasting energy because if we don't know where we want to go, we will never get there, as the Cat tells Alice:

"Would you tell me, please, which way I ought to go from here?"

"That depends a good deal on where you want to get to," the Cheshire Cat told her.

"I don't much care where," said Alice.

"Then it doesn't much matter which way you go," the Cat said.

"...So long as I get somewhere", added Alice as an explanation.

"Oh, you're sure to do that if only you walk long enough."

Surely, in whatever direction we go, we'll get somewhere, but we won't get where we want to be unless we get there by chance, and it is not good for us to just leave it to luck because, most of the time, we won't enjoy where it ultimately took us. And as time is irreversible, we will figure out at one point that time has passed without us getting where we wanted to be.

In addition to that, setting a goal also has an important psychological effect as it equips us with patience and determination; while reaching the closeness to our goal impels us.

At the same time, it is great to set intermediate goals for at least two reasons:

1. From a psychological point of view, focusing exclusively on the major goal can be overwhelming; it seems so far away and hard to reach, it can overwhelm us, and we could abandon the race.

2. As a famous Chinese proverb says, "a journey of a thousand miles begins with the a single step." In other words, it is good not to think too far away and to begin taking shorter stages, which are easily manageable. Achieving these stage goals will propel us. We will see that the road is not as difficult and that, as we went through the previous stages, we can go through the next ones until the fulfillment of our vision.

I will give you an example of a personality that I admire a lot as a sportswoman as well as a human being, Simona Halep, the Romanian tennis champion. I've seen many interviews with her, and almost all of them emphasize this point: focusing on one target close and relatively easy to reach, as she says, "I take things step by step."

At the beginning of each tournament, she sets her vision, which is represented by winning the tournament, but once she does that, she "forgets" about it and sets the goal to win the next match, then, once the match starts, she sets the goal of winning the game that starts, and once the game begins, she aims to win the point she plays.

Of course, the final goal remains unchanged, but it is like a guiding light. We look at it from time to time to make sure that we haven't lost our direction, but we have to be careful not to hit the nearby rocks that can sink the ship.

During the journey to fulfill the vision, the road can meander; sometimes obstacles can appear, and we have to go around avoiding them or run late, depending on the concrete conditions that we encounter.

That's why it's good for us to set short-term goals that we can reach quickly and, if the situation requires, change them slightly.

I have seen a comparison of the road to fulfilling our vision with the 2,900 mile road from New York to San Francisco, which I really enjoyed and which I find very suggestive: if we go by car, at night, we do not need to see more than the headlights allows us because as long as we know where we want to go and follow the signs, we will reach the destination, even if we only see a few hundred yards ahead of us.

This comparison seems suggestive to me because the vision is the destination where we want to end up at the end of the journey, and the map is the plan that we have in mind. A prudent traveler will set his stopping points for refueling, to rest, to eat, and possibly even to admire certain objectives (we must also enjoy the trip, don't we?), and if necessary, we can change the route, keeping the direction in mind, focusing, however, on what we have to do in the short term.

An important tool in fulfilling the vision is visualization.

We simply imagine where we want to go and what we want to achieve. Visualization keeps us excited, keeps us focused, and has the "miraculous" tendency to be fulfilled.

Many of you have probably seen the movie "The Secret" (if you haven't seen it, I recommend it, it's on Netflix) or you've read the book, or in any case, you've heard of the Law of Attraction. It is an empirical law, but from one's own experience and the confessions of many people, it works.

This Law of Attraction says that whatever we deeply desire and we visualize, the Universe will do so in order for us to acquire it.

There is no magic here; it is simply about triggering some psychological mechanisms that help us become more attentive to opportunities that appear along the way in connection with what we actually want. Things that would have happened unnoticed before, now we notice them, and we just have the impression that it is a coincidence.

I'm sure it happened to you more than once to think about a certain person you haven't seen in a while or haven't talked with in a long time, and in the next few days you meet him/her or find out news about him/her. It's all a consequence of the Law of Attraction; it's probably about energy waves, telepathy (science can't explain it) that made thoughts "to materialize." Think hard, and you will surely remember that something similar happened to you in the past.

There is a famous example of the power of visualization: the great basketball player Michael Jordan, who, being asked how he manages to score so many times and to create so many spectacular passes, said that he repeats them daily, thousands of times, in his mind.

Visualization "tricks" the brain into acknowledging that the action actually takes place, and through repeated visualizations, neural pathways are created for the muscles respectively, which act with increased precision.

A very eloquent example of visualization is that of Martin Luther King, with his famous speech, "I have a dream." A dream represents images, in other words, visualization. He imagined the world he wished for, a world that, for many, seemed impossible to achieve.

As Simon Sinek, the well-known author and motivational speaker, said, Dr. King told us, "I have a dream, not, I have a plan," emphasizing the importance of visualization in achieving the vision.

Many people may feel that it is simple to visualize: simply imagine something, a car, for example, and then, in a few days, maybe they will receive it. But it is not that simple: it is necessary to visualize it as precise and detailed as possible. We need to clearly see the brand of the car, the model, the color, the interior, the color of the seats, the equipment, the smell, imagining that we are behind the wheel driving it, that we move the steering wheel, that we accelerate, to have the feeling we are in the car. The more detailed the visualization is, the stronger the processes triggered in the brain are, which will make us pay more attention to things that have to do with the object of the visualization, which we overlooked before.

To realize the power and importance of vision and visualization, I will tell you Monty Edwards' story: Monty Edwards was born into a family without money, his father was a horse trainer, and his job made him relocate from one horse ranch to another, so Monty changed schools often.

At one of the schools, the teacher asked him to write an essay about what he wants to become when he grows up. The boy did not hesitate at all and wrote seven pages about owning a horse farm, describing, in great detail, how the buildings will look like and even he draw the plan of the house.

Two days later, he received the lowest grade, F. When he asked the teacher why she gave him this grade, she replied that his writing was fanciful, that it is impossible for him, from a family without any resources, to become the owner of a horse ranch.

Asking his father what to do, whether to exchange his paper for a higher grade or to remain true to his vision but remain low-grade, his father replied that this decision is very important and that it had to be carefully considered.

Monty went to the teacher two days later and said, *"Keep the F and I will keep my dream!"*

He ended up with a 200-acre horse ranch and a 4000-square-foot house.

He kept his minimum grade essay for all of his life, and he still has it framed on the wall.

Napoleon Hill strongly recommends visualization as a habit when we lie in bed while we fall asleep because then, in that state of semi-consciousness, thoughts enter deeply into the subconscious mind.

There are studies that show that when we are about to fall asleep, the area of the brain responsible for critical thinking has low activity, while the area responsible for creativity is highly active. So, critical thinking is not awake and does not "tell" us that our visualization is just a dream, a fantasy, that we have no chance of materializing it; instead, the area responsible for creativity is active, creating visualizations, dreams, feeding and stimulating our subconscious mind with the visualization of what we desire.

Visualization helps us in many situations, and I have the example of one person very close and dear to me, who, nine years ago, was diagnosed with a very serious disease, acute leukemia. The doctors' prognosis was reserved, only 3 to 6 months. Consequently, she started treatment, which was very aggressive, among other serious side effects being insomnia.

Trying to fall asleep, lying in bed, she began to think fairy tales, childhood fairy tales, which, for the most part, had as main character Prince Charming - the positive character and the Dragon- the negative character, leading a continuous struggle. How she couldn't sleep, she began to slowly lengthen them to complicate them; she began to identify herself with Prince Charming and the disease, with the Dragon. Every night, the two of them fought, and Prince Charming came out victorious every single time.

There were many such nights in which she defeated leukemia, every time Prince Charming defeated the Dragon. She literally saw how her own body fights the disease and wins.

In the end, she won the fight, and she still lives today. She is healthy, and she is enjoying her life, her family, her children, and her grandchildren. This story is about my mother!

Coming back to Simona Halep's example, she said how her father, Mr. Stere Halep, believed a lot in her, encouraged her, and supported her, always telling her that she would win a Grand Slam.

This shows that Mr. Halep had a vision. He imagined his daughter, and he visualized her becoming a Grand Slam champion. Without this vision, it would have been difficult to think that he would admit that Simona, who started tennis at an early age to have a lifestyle with many restrictions, would become a Grand Slam champion and that he would have made the efforts and the material sacrifices necessary for her to succeed in tennis, without having any guarantee.

The supreme example of visualization and its power is that of the great inventor Nikola Tesla: he imagined his inventions in the smallest detail and visualized complicated mechanisms. Then, he proceeded to their realization without even drawing sketches.

Finally, a warning: it is not easy to visualize the smallest details concerning the object of the vision, as it requires an effort of concentration, because thoughts are very volatile, they tend to be quickly replaced by other thoughts, unrelated to what we want to visualize.

Anyone who is under the impression that visualization is simple is wrong because it requires effort, focus, focus on the subject, and training. So, it is important to visualize as frequently as you can, and over time, it will become easier and easier, until ultimately, it becomes a reflex.

"Vision gets us in motion; determination leads us to the end."

COMMITMENT

"Commitment means staying loyal to what you said you were going to do long after the mood you said it in has left you."

Orebela Gbenga

If vision is the poetic part of the road to success, then commitment and perseverance represent the heroic part, the effort, your "blood, sweat and tears".

If we have a vision and we visualize it, but we don't make the necessary effort to achieve it, it will be in vain, and we won't achieve anything.

There are two great dangers that hover and prevent many to begin or complete the journey to vision.

Procrastination

There are some people that are constantly waiting for the right time to take action, in other words waiting for the stars to "align."

It is, in fact, the fear of throwing oneself into the unknown, the fear of not being made fun of ("what will my family say? what will my friends say?"), fear of failure.

They hide this fear under the pretext of waiting for the right time, the passage of the economic crisis, the improvement of the economic climate, the promulgation of a law that would bring facilities in the field in which they want to launch, etc.

Thus, they postpone day after day, week after week, month after month, until they come to a conclusion that "it's too late, I missed the train." It's the situation of someone who wants to lose a few pounds and can't start today, because it's an anniversary, also not tomorrow, because the wife cooked his favorite meal and so on.

In this situation, the only solution is to cut the Gordian knot and immediately take action. No textbook or teacher can teach us that; it simply takes an effort of will.

No one can help us, we are the only ones that can trigger the action, the only ones who can take matter in our own hands and throw ourselves into the water, we are the only ones who can jump on things.

I went through this situation before writing this book, which I've wanted to write for a while, but I postponed it on and on because I didn't have the time, I had other pressing things to solve, I didn't have a clearly established plan, I didn't know what I was going to write, doubting if someone was interested in what I was going to write, concerned that I was going to make a fool of myself, that I will write it in vain, that there are already many books that deal with this subject. Just a handful of reasons to postpone.

The trigger was my niece, who had written several interesting articles and asked for my help to publish a book based on those articles. I helped her. I got very involved in that project, the book was very good, and it ultimately inspired me.

So, after I had finished the project and her book was published, on a Wednesday morning, around 9:30, I told myself, "enough, this is the moment." I simply got on my computer, opened a Word file, and started writing, based on a minimal plan, meaning that I knew what topic I wanted to tackle and the five points I wanted the book to contain. It was incredible how words started to come by me. I wrote at a brisk pace. I didn't need to think; my ideas were simply flowing, sometimes even faster than I could write. Of course, the stage of the finishing touches and correcting errors will follow, but the essence was written the first time.

Negligence

The second danger is neglect, which occurs overtime during the journey to vision.

We managed to overcome the difficulty to start, but, as we went on, we thought that it was too hard, that we weren't getting near the purpose, that there are too many obstacles which we did not foresee, that we would not be able to reach the final goal, regardless how much effort we put in and that we better give up sooner than later, so as not to spend energy, time and money without getting any result.

You know the expression "born as a talent and died as a hope." It is said about someone who had all the conditions to succeed, but which, for various reasons, he/she didn't reach his/her full potential because, somewhere along the way, he/she lost himself/herself. There are many such examples, the most visible being from sports.

Of course, there are different situations. We may not have anticipated all the difficulties, and indeed, it is not worth consuming energy, time, and money for an unachievable goal. But we must reach this conclusion only after we make a serious analysis when we are 100%

sure that this is the real conclusion and not the result of neglect, boredom, tiredness, or lack of enthusiasm because we can't achieve our desired results faster.

If the analysis shows us that it is better to reorient ourselves, it is better to change the direction, but, mandatorily we must set a new goal so we stay focused. With these changes, there is a big danger to postpone the resumption of the race.

The antidote to these dangers, procrastination and neglect is commitment, which is the pledge we take to ourselves that we will finish the journey to the final purpose.

We must realize that the journey is not easy and there are difficulties ahead, but that is to our advantage. If it were easy, we would have had fierce competition, as there would have been many tempted to take the same journey in order to reach the same goal.

It is to our advantage, but only if we show determination and desire to succeed in reaching the end of the journey.

When I say determination, the first example of which I can think of is Hellen Keller, who, at the age of 19 months, lost her sight and hearing due to an illness.

However, through an extraordinary determination, she was able to learn to speak, write and read, with the help of Ann Sullivan, who is another example of exceptional determination. She then attended various schools and graduated from Harvard University, becoming the first person without sight and hearing to obtain a university degree.

She became a renowned author, writing 14 books and hundreds of essays and speeches on various topics, from animals to Mahatma Gandhi.

Helen Keller started life with a handicap, and the condition was considered insurmountable. Still, she imagined herself getting to another level, far exceeding her theoretical chances, and managed to do so only by determination.

Ramón Arroyo was an ordinary man, husband, and father, with a normal job, whose life was turned upside down when he was diagnosed with multiple sclerosis, a disease that affected his capacity to move. But, his dream was to take part in the triathlon Ironman, a very tough sporting event consisting of swimming a distance of 3.86 km, followed by a bicycle race of 180 km, and finally, running a distance of 42 km.

Helped by his father-in-law, Ramón started training. The seizures continued, making the training really difficult. He had moments in which he wanted to abandon it, telling himself that there was no point and that he is too ill to succeed. But, he clenched his teeth, he continued, and in the end, he signed up for the race. Even if he had great difficulties, he finished it, becoming the first person with multiple sclerosis that managed to pass the finish line in an Ironman triathlon. In the following years, he participated and finished many other races, proving that no obstacle is insurmountable if there is determination.

Corina Morariu is a former American tennis player of Romanian origin. At the age of 23, being at her peak, she was diagnosed with a rare and severe form of leukemia. She underwent a series of very aggressive chemotherapy treatments, which weakened her significantly. She was close to abandoning the therapy due to her condition. Helped by her family, she managed to overcome this obstacle, completed the treatment, fortunately with excellent results and healing, but remaining with a state of fatigue and weakness.

She had the wish to continue playing tennis, so she resumed practice and got back on the pitch, managing to get in the doubles final of the Melbourne Grand Slam tournament. Many would probably have been satisfied that they managed to overcome a relentless disease and would not continue to make the necessary effort for high-performance sports. Still, Corina was determined to resume her work at the top level, becoming an example for many athletes.

As Andy Andrews rightly said, "When confrunted with a challenge, the commited heart will search for a solution. The undecided heart searches for an escape."

It's not easy, it never is, and there will be temptations all the time. An inner voice will always tell us, "Come on, it's not the end of the world if you take a break." I'm not saying that we shouldn't have moments of relaxation; they are more than necessary, but not to prolong them and become the rule and the moments of action to become just that, "moments."

As the quote at the beginning of the chapter, *"Commitment means staying loyal to what you said you were going to do long after the mood you said it in has left you."*

It is 100% correct because, during the journey, the enthusiasm of the beginning disappears, when we were convinced that we could move mountains and that nothing could be too difficult. Along the way, difficulties arise, and just when we need more enthusiasm, it disappears. In these moments, we need determination, which gives us the strength to continue when we struggle, when we feel like giving up.

Determination is what makes us clench our teeth and try again and again until we get the desired result.

I'm sure you all know Nick Vujicic, who was born without his lower and upper limbs: it was certainly not easy for him, but the fact that he was determined made him succeed, and today he is a very successful man. He is thriving as a family man, in his profession, and also financially. He is one of the great motivational speakers and authors and also a source of inspiration for many people.

It would have been easy for him to say that he was unlucky and indulge in an assisted existence, and no one would have condemned him, they would have even approved him, but he set a goal, he had a vision, which he achieved by determination.

I am convinced that he had hard times, moments when he felt like giving up everything, but his determination made him move on. And here's how far he has come!

Nick's achievements must make us realize that no obstacle, of any kind, is too great, that it cannot be overcome or avoided. If Nick has succeeded at this level, then we have no excuses or reasons not to succeed!

Let us keep in mind and guide ourselves by Nick's saying:

"The challenges in our lives are to strengthen our beliefs. They don't have the role in overwhelming us."

As a former great tennis player, Billie Jean King said, *"Pressure is a privilege,"* referring to the pressure we encounter as we play at a high level. She referred to tennis, but it is valid in any domain. If there is no pressure, it means that there is no stake. If something is too easy to achieve, it means that there is no reward. So, we must be grateful when we feel pressure. It means that we care, that the effort is not in vain, and that it is worthwhile to be determined to go through the journey to the end.

When we feel that it is difficult for us to continue, we should think of those future mothers who have problems with pregnancy and who, in order not to lose the child, have to stay in bed for months, practically without leaving it. I can't even imagine what level of determination these women have, what strength of character they show. Compared to their sacrifice, almost anything else can look like a walk in the park!

Another example of determination is represented by those women who, in order to have children, undergo difficult and painful treatments (periodic injections, surgical interventions, a lot of unpleasant examinations) for months, even years, everything to fulfill their dream, that of giving birth. Without a limitless determination, they would not succeed!

You've probably all heard of the great physicist and cosmologist Stephen Hawking. He was diagnosed in his youth, at only 21 years old, with a disabling and incurable neurological disease, amyotrophic lateral sclerosis. This disease progressively affected his muscles so that he could no longer use his limbs, and in the end, he could not even speak.

However, he continued to be a scientist with remarkable achievements, having a prodigious activity spanning over several decades. Only an extraordinary determination made this "miracle" possible.

Finally, I want to emphasize one thing: we must differentiate between desire and determination. We can want many things. Desire can be an essential catalyst on the road to the established goal, but desire alone is often not enough. Determination is what always leads us to the end.

Desire can be abandoned without consequences because there will be other opportunities, but determination makes abandonment impossible.

I found on LinkedIn a story about determination, on Digamber Kumar's account, which is very suggestive:

"A little boy notices how the cat sees a mouse and prepares to catch it to eat it. The mouse also sees the cat, realizes the danger, and runs away. There follows a race that seems to have the cat as the winner. The mouse does not give up and manages, at the last moment, to find a hole in which to hide."

The boy asks his father:

"How come the cat, even though it was bigger, stronger, and faster, couldn't catch the mouse?"

"Because the cat just wanted to eat, while the mouse was determined to save its life. For the cat, it was not the end of the world that it did not eat; it will have other opportunities; instead, for the mouse, there was nothing to choose from."

"Did you win? Keep going! Did you lose? Keep going!"

Pierre de Coubertin

PERSEVERANCE

"Going on one more round, when you don't think you can, that's what makes all the difference."

Sylvester Stallone

If determination is the fuel, then perseverance is the engine.

The two go hand in hand. If we have one, it is in vain if it is not accompanied by the other.

We can have the best engine, but if we do not refuel it, it will standstill. We can also have the tank full, but if the engine is missing or broken, we will not be able to advance even an inch.

Perseverance is the one that makes it possible to express determination.

It is perseverance that makes us try again and again, and the next day to start over.

The road to vision is not easy; there are many obstacles, some we have foreseen, but most of them, we didn't, we often have doubts, not knowing if we will succeed or fail.

Here I feel the need to make a clarification, which emphasizes that, in fact, there is no failure: if we follow our vision, even if we do not achieve it, it does not mean that we have not achieved anything. During the journey, we get some intermediate results; we reach some milestones, which can be starting points for another purpose, solid bases for a new journey, which can be lessons for what we have to do better, lessons about what we must avoid.

As Norman Vincent Peale said:

"Shoot for the moon. Even if you miss, you'll land among the stars."

But all this is possible only if we persevere, only if we are willing to make an extra effort, if we give 101%, and go beyond our comfort zone.

Perseverance is what makes a parent who comes home tired after a day of work, and all he wants is to relax, to stand up when the child asks him/her for help with his/her homework because he/she did not understand something, and to do this each evening because he/she has the vision of a good future for the child and is determined to help him/her achieve that future.

I saw a very good movie, "Hacksaw Ridge," about a real case from World War II, in which the main character manages to save dozens of wounded soldiers, carrying them on his back, one by one, up to the field hospital.

He did this a lot of times, and every time he brought a comrade to the hospital, he prayed that he could bring another one. He continued to save his colleagues, although, by all standards, he had no chance, being under enemy fire and having to climb and descend a hill with a wounded man on his back. The effort should have brought him down after the first 2-3 trips, but just as Sylvester Stallone said, the difference was his ability to make another trip, even when he thought it was no longer possible. His perseverance saved the lives of dozens of people.

There is no recipe for perseverance. In fact, it is a simple recipe, available to anyone:

"*Have you succeeded? Keep going! Have you failed? Keep going!*" as Pierre de Coubertin said.

That's what Edison did when he invented the electric bulb. On that occasion, a reporter took the following interview (from my memory):

"*Mister Edison, how did you succeed inventing the light bulb?*"

"*I tried 10,000 materials until I found one that didn't melt and made light. This material was the one that fulfilled both conditions*", answered Edison.

"*So, you failed 9,999 times until you managed to find the right material?*" the reporter asked.

"*No, I found 9,999 materials which are not right for this purpose*", Edison said.

So, it depends on the perspective from which we see things.

If Edison had considered, like the reporter and probably, like most people, that every failed attempt is a failure, he would have given up at some point. However, Edison had the vision of the light bulb. He was determined to get work done, and he had the perseverance to continue until he reached his goal.

Probably not many of you know who is Mihaela Buzărnescu, the Romanian tennis player, whose story is inspiring: after a very promising career in juniors, she switched to professional tennis, only that, right at the beginning, she had a series of health problems that prevented her from achieving the expected results. As one problem was solved, another soon appeared, and this fragmentation did not allow her adequate preparation. As such, she took a break from tennis for several years until she was sure she had solved her problems.

She returned to the circuit at the age of 29, an age at which many players end their careers, and returned with real success, achieving many notable results, including winning a tournament and reaching 20th place in the WTA rankings.

It was perseverance that made her not give up, being able to resume her career "against all odds," although it seemed extremely unlikely to succeed.

Her vision and determination gave her the strength to start over, and her perseverance gave her the strength to practice every day, without any guarantee that the efforts would pay off.

Why is it important to persevere, even when or especially when we think there is no point in continuing? Because success may be "right around the corner."

I read a story that took place during the California Gold Rush in the mid-nineteenth century, about a gold digger who bought a small plot of land and began digging, hoping to enrich himself. The time passed, and he had found nothing. The money was running out, and the discouragement had reached its peak, so he decided to sell the land and tools and go in search of other opportunities. The story goes that the one who bought the plot of land reached gold after the first blows of the pickaxe and got rich. If the first seeker had persevered, he would have got rich.

A proof of perseverance is the American writer, John Grisham. He was a lawyer; he made a good living. He lived a good life by all standards, but his dream was to become a writer, so he wrote a book, a legal thriller, "A time to kill" (I'm sure many of you have read it, it's an excellent book).

It took him four years to write it, it is a book with complicated action, with many characters, with a narrative on several levels, so it was a difficult book to write, especially for a novice author. Still, Grisham was not discouraged by the long time it took to write it, so he persevered until he finished it.

He sent it to several publishing houses, and absolutely all of them, 28 in number, rejected it. Not only did they reject it, but they also discouraged him, telling him that the genre was not wanted, that it has no public appeal, and that, if he wants to write, he should try another genre.

Maybe 99% of the writers would have been discouraged, the "experts" said that their work would not be successful.

John Grisham, however, had a vision, and that vision was that he would be successful as author of legal thrillers. Still, he also had perseverance, which led him to send the manuscript to another publishing house, a small one, which agreed to publish a number of 5,000 copies.

As the publishing house was small, it didn't have the resources to promote the book, so Grisham, at his own expense, filled his trunk with books and went to various book fairs to try to sell them.

The rest is history: the first book was followed by a series of 28 consecutive bestsellers, sold in 300 million copies, from which eight were made movies with top stars, Tom Cruise, Julia Roberts, Denzel Washington, Tommy Lee Jones, Susan Sarandon, bringing him millions of dollars in royalties and made hundreds of millions of dollars in revenue.

John Grisham's example reminds me of another important point: first of all, we must rely on our judgment and instinct and not on the opinions of experts.

The experts cannot feel what we feel; they do not know the situation as we do. They judge from a conservative point of view, according to the conclusions drawn from their experience. It is good to listen carefully to what they have to say, precisely because they have solid knowledge in the field and a rich experience, but everything must pass through our filter, and we should not consider their words as gospel.

Did you know, for example, that 98% of manuscripts sent to publishers are rejected (including John Grisham's first manuscript or the first volume in the Harry Potter series - incredible, right?)

An amazing example of rejection in music is the album "A night at the Opera" by Queen!

Why do you think those manuscripts are rejected, and why can't people with significant experience "smell" the potential success? Because people have a natural tendency to protect themselves, not to take risks, and avoid leaving their comfort zone.

Both John Grisham and J.K. Rowling were on their first try. They were completely unknown authors, and the publishers did not want to take risks, to make a fool of themselves, and even possibly lose their jobs due to the failures that could have occurred by publishing these volumes.

In the case of Queen, although at that time the band was already famous, "A night at the Opera" was something very different from what was played at the time, and the record company did not have the courage to launch it. If it weren't for Freddie's perseverance and his bandmates, the world would have been deprived of a masterpiece.

An example of great perseverance is also represented by the former Croatian tennis player, Goran Ivanisevic, who, until the age of 30, had reached second place on the ATP. He even played a Grand Slam final but lost it to Andre Agassi. Many players would have thought they had an outstanding career, but Goran's dream was to win a Grand Slam. At the age of 30, he was ranked 126th in the ATP rankings, and everyone considered him "finished." Probably other players would have retired, but he did not give up his dream, considering that he would have another chance.

And the chance came in 2001 when he received a wild card to play at Wimbledon. And what seemed inconceivable to many, actually happened, as he won the tournament, being the first holder of a wild card to win this Grand Slam tournament. I remember him at the awards ceremony and how happy he was. If he hadn't persevered in such manner, he would have regretted it for his whole life, that he did not try his chance to the very end.

I don't know if you saw the movie "The Founder" about the life of Ray Kroc, the one who made McDonald's what it is today, a multinational company. Until the age of 50, Ray tried all kinds of businesses, especially as a salesman, traveling thousands of miles every month, trying to sell all kinds of equipment to restaurant owners.

I won't go into details, but at the age of 50, he had the opportunity to open a fast-food restaurant, which didn't go well at first. Still, Ray had the patience and perseverance to continue until he found the winning formula. He himself said that the only quality that made him succeed was perseverance.

Andre Agassi was a wonder child of tennis, exploding at the age of 16, but as time went by, he failed to win a Grand Slam tournament, the dream of any tennis player. He lost three dramatic finals, and in all of them, he was considered to have the best odds. But all this did not discourage him. On the contrary, they were reasons to persevere, and when the next opportunity arose, the fourth final, he defeated Goran Ivanisevic, about whom I told you earlier. This was followed by seven more Grand Slam tournament wins, an Olympic title, and a prodigious career. All those merits are due to the fact that he persevered; he did not give up and was not filled with despair after "failures."

And when I say perseverance, I mean "Colonel Sanders," the legendary founder of Kentucky Fried Chicken, "KFC," who started his business at the age of 65, when most people retire Still, he started the business of his life, his dream being to popularize his sauce, which is famous today. And the success was complete, under the KFC logo operating today over 22,000 restaurants in 150 countries.

These are all famous examples, but there are many others that we know personally, each of us, people who have achieved remarkable things, precisely because they did not give up and continued, even if at some point they seemed to have no chance. Think hard; you probably know someone!

"The critical part of finding balance in life is choosing priorities"

Byron Pulsifier

BALANCE

"Balance isn't something you achieve someday."

Nick Vujicic

Balance is essential in order to enjoy reaching our goals.

Suppose determination and perseverance are indispensable for fulfilling the vision. In that case, balance is necessary in order for the road to be pleasant, and once the goal is reached, to feel fulfilled, not exhausted by the effort, and able to enjoy the victory.

It is known that "too much of anything is bad".

It's good to have determination and perseverance, but we must not lose sight of the big picture, namely that we must enjoy the journey, feel good, and not make those close to us suffer.

It is pointless to have a vision, to have determination and perseverance if we are not interested in the wellbeing of those around us, especially our families. After all, they should also be the beneficiaries of our success. It must be seen in a broad sense as a fulfillment on all levels, including or especially family. If the attainment of the vision, of the goal, estranges us from our loved ones, what is its purpose? If we do not keep our balance, surely, sooner or later, our health is also affected and, again, isn't the price of "success" too high?

There are many known cases of people who achieved financial and professional success but ended up alone or in poor health because of the years in which they pursued only one thing, neglecting their families and/or their health.

I do not think that this kind of success is desirable, nor do I think that we can call it a success.

It is not easy to maintain this balance at all times because our vision can capture all our attention. We are passionate; we enter autopilot, not being able to realize that the distance between our family and us is slowly increasing or that health problems may occur.

We start deceiving ourselves, we find excuses, "after all, I sacrifice myself for the family, they should understand that," when in fact those arguments are just excuses that, even if they are sincere, they do not improve the situation at all. If financial or professional success were enough, there would not be so many cases of broken families and children estranged from their parents, suicides, drug use in people who, by accepted standards, are being "successful."

The funny thing is that maintaining a balance even helps achieve our vision because a healthy family environment, a happy family, favors a state of mind for dealing with the effort. We can more easily endure an intense effort, a stressful situation, if we have balance at home and if we have friends whom we spend pleasant moments with. Even if we do not realize it, a state of tension or even just indifference at home hurts and affects us. We cannot function optimally in conditions of prolonged stress.

It is like a very good car that is continuously pushed to its limits so that at some point, something fails, and it is much more difficult to repair it than would have been to prevent it by reasonable use.

There are ways in which we can determine a balance between the various aspects of life.

We need to set clear boundaries between personal and family life, and professional life.

For example, we can set a reasonable daily time limit when we stop working and we stop thinking about professional issues.

We also set a day, even two days a week, in which we dedicate our full time to family activities.

Also, we make sure we take vacation at least once a year.

All these are, as I said, beneficial for the professional side. They provide an escape, a break from the routine, which refreshes our brain and increases our efficiency at work.

Of course, there may be situations in which we have to deal with professional problems in our free time, but we have to be careful that those situations are exceptions and they are not meant to increase in frequency. They should not take course over an extensive period of time and do not become the rule.

The basic principle in these situations should be, "can those situations wait until tomorrow/until Monday/until I return from my vacation?" If yes, then it can most definitely wait!

The good part is that although it may seem difficult to maintain balance, as we practice, it becomes easier and easier, and we will achieve it naturally.

It's just like riding a bike. It's hard until we learn how to do it, then it becomes a reflex, we don't forget it all our lives and we practice it without even thinking about it.

Essentially, balance means setting our priorities in place.

I found this story extremely suggestive about maintaining the balance between various components of life. Many of you have probably read it, but it is still worth saying:

"One day, a teacher comes into the classroom with an empty jar, then he fills it with some large stones and asks the students:

"*Is the jar full?*"

"*It is,*" the students replied.

The teacher began to put little tiny stones into the jar until it became full.

"*Is the jar full?*" the teacher asked again.

"*It is,*" the students replied again.

The teacher then started to pour sand into the jar until it was full.

"*Is the jar full now?*" the teacher asked again.

"*It is,*" the students replied.

"*I want you to imagine,*" the professor continued, "*that this jar is your life: stones are the most important things in your life, family, health, moral principles. The little tiny stones are the other things that matter: career, money, house, car. And the sand is the small, most unimportant thing.*

If you put sand in the jar first, there will be no room for little stones and larger stones. So, pay close attention to the things that matter most to you: spend time with your family, always keep your health in mind and don't ever neglect it, do not forget to flourish your spirit, be kind, honest, sensitive, empathetic. These are the most important things, the ones that matter and should be a top priority. The rest is just sand."

In a study conducted in Australia concerning patients on the verge of death, they were asked what they regretted most in life and what would be the first thing they would change if they could, and the majority's answer was *"insufficient time spent with my family."*

We need to make sure that financial or professional success does not become goals, but really be just the means by which we can ensure a better life for the family, we have to be sure that this life includes us and we are not just a source of money, because our family nor we will really enjoy them.

We are like a juggler with several balls (family, job, health, friends), and we must be careful not to lose sight of any one of them and ultimately not to end up destroying them.

"Gratitude is a powerfull catalyst for happiness. It's the spark that lights a fire of joy in your soul."

Amy Collette

GRATITUDE

"Gratitude makes sense of our past, brings peace for today, and creates a vision for tomorrow."

Melody Beattie

At the end of the day, when we have achieved our vision and reached our goals, it is imperative to keep our head clear and our feet on the ground, not to think that we are more important than we are.

The best way to keep our composure is to be grateful to those who helped us, to those who were with us during the journey. Moreover, we must publicly give them the credit that they deserve and be aware that we, alone, would not have succeeded and let them feel that their merits are recognized.

Most of the time, or maybe even every time, success is a team effort, each member of the team has its role, without which, very possibly, the mechanism would have seized or would not have worked so well, and success would not have appeared or reach its full potential.

In addition to those who actually participated in the effort, we must also show gratitude to those who participated indirectly in our success, the most important being family members, our spouses, our children, who were understanding, who were attentive to us, who created all the conditions for us at home to be able to focus as much as possible on what we had to do.

We must be grateful to those who contributed to our evolution; without whom, we would not have been the person we are. So we would not have had the success that we managed to achieve.

Therefore, we must be grateful to our parents, siblings, and all the mentors we have had, from teachers to formal or informal mentors, that life has brought in our way. It is also proper to be grateful even to those who did not like us, who did not treat us well, to those who, perhaps, wronged us because they showed us how we should not behave with others.

We should also be grateful to our friends because they enrich our lives, because they are with us throughout the happiest and the least happy moments.

And last but not least, we must be grateful to the Universe, to God, to the Universal Energy, to Mother Nature or whatever you call it because it gives us the energy to start the day with, it gave us the family that we have, and it gave us the friends that we have.

It is excellent to have a daily ritual of gratitude, to express it in intimacy. Thus, we become aware that alone we can't do anything or only very little, and thus we do not become arrogant.

Then, it is good that, from time to time, we express our gratitude to our loved ones, best with our deeds, to let them see that we are grateful to them, that we also take care of them, that we protect them, just as they have taken care of us and our needs.

Anthony Ray Hinton's story is a telling example of the power of gratitude.

Anthony was sentenced to death for a crime he didn't commit and spent 30 years on death row, awaiting execution. Eventually, the truth was brought to light, and the Supreme Court released him.

Upon his release from prison, Anthony said:

"One does not know the value of freedom until it is taken away, People run out of the rain. I run into the rain…I am so grateful for every drop. Just to feel it on my face."

He also said:

"I wake up in the morning and I don't need anyone to make me laugh. I'm going to laugh on my own, because I have been blessed to see another day, and when you're blessed to see another day that should automatically give you joy."

If we are not grateful for what we have, we risk not getting what we want.

Gratitude works hand in hand with the Law of Attraction: if we want something and then, after receiving what we wanted, we are not grateful, the next time we want anything, most likely, we will not receive it.

But gratitude must be real, from the bottom of the heart and not faked. We, in our souls, know if we are grateful only to show others that we are or because we feel it inside of us.

In the most difficult times that we are experiencing (or we think we are experiencing), even in those moments, we must be grateful for what we have.

As Hellen Keller put it:

"I cried because I had no shoes. Then I met a man who had no feet."

There are studies which show that the expression of gratitude contributes to the achievement of a state of well-being, which, in turn, helps us to have a higher yield in whatever we undertake.

We can express our gratitude by a simple "thank you" said to the cashier at the supermarket, by turning on the emergency lights to show appreciation to the ones that let us enter a crowded intersection, although we had no priority. It's simple, it takes a few seconds, but it's worth it.

Let me give you another example, starring Simona Halep: in 2014, then WTA CEO, Stacey McAllister, told a story from 2013 after the final of a tournament won by Simona. The match ended quite late, followed by the awards ceremony; then, the players followed the recovery procedure after the match. So they arrived at the hotel at around 11 pm.

Although it was late and she was tired after the effort, Simona gave Mrs. McAllister an e-mail thanking her for the conditions provided and expressed her gratitude for the beautiful words she said about her at the awards ceremony.

"*She was the only player I ever received such an email from,*" said Mrs. McAllister (quoted from memory).

This last example demonstrates what Dale Carnegie said in his famous book, "How to win friends and influence people," that it's best to never wait for someone's gratitude, because if it doesn't come, we won't be disappointed, and if it does, the happier we will be.

This is why it is good to be grateful and to express our gratitude because the person will be even more pleasantly surprised.

"All good things come to an end."

Nelly Furtado

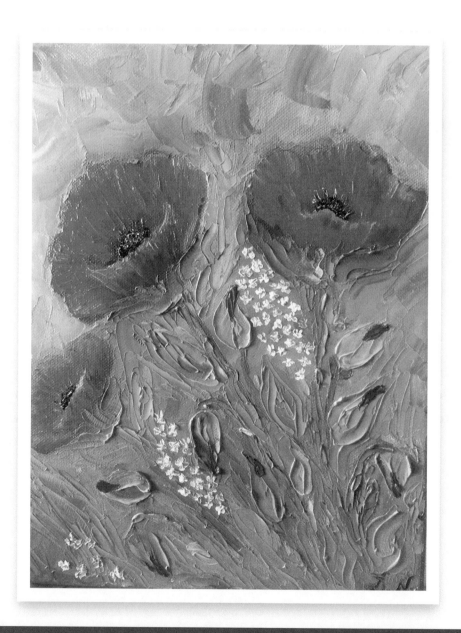

CLOSURE

You have reached the end of this book, and it made me very happy to write it: I had it inside of me for some time, but I couldn't bring it to the surface.

I thank everyone who took the time to read my thoughts. I hope you find them valuable and exciting.

I am grateful to you because, although I already consider this book a success for me (I had its vision, I had the determination and perseverance to finish it, and I kept the balance between the time and effort allocated to it and other activities), the fact that there are readers (many, few, it doesn't matter), makes this success even more enjoyable.

I will be very grateful if you will send me your thoughts and impressions at dr.drcip@gmail.com

At last, I send my thoughts of gratitude, especially to Delia, my wife, and our two children, who have been with me in this adventure and have always encouraged me. To my parents, who have an important contribution to who I am today. To the other members of my extended family, with whom I have a wonderful relationship, and to the friends who were with me when I needed them.

March 2021

"If your dreams don't scare you, it means they are too small"

Richard Branson

Printed in the United States
by Baker & Taylor Publisher Services